A REPUBLIC OF LINEN

Patrick Brandon was born in London in 1965. A recipient of a New Writing Ventures bursary in 2006, he won the Essex Poetry Prize 2005, and received commendations in the Wigtown Poetry Prize 2005, and in the National Poetry Competition 2007. He studied painting at Norwich School of Art, and has exhibited regularly in the Royal Academy Summer Exhibition. In 2003 he was shortlisted for the Jerwood Drawing Prize. He currently works as a Technician at the Tate. He lives in London with his partner and two young children.

18th July 2009

Patrick Brandon

A **REPUBLIC** OF
LINEN

To Fran & Bernie,
with love

Patrick

BLOODAXE BOOKS

ISBN: 978 1 85224 855 0

First published 2009 by
Bloodaxe Books Ltd,
Highgreen,
Tarset,
Northumberland NE48 1RP.

www.bloodaxebooks.com
For further information about Bloodaxe titles
please visit our website or write to
the above address for a catalogue.

Supported by
**ARTS COUNCIL
ENGLAND**

Cover design: Neil Astley & Pamela Robertson-Pearce.

Printed in Great Britain by
Bell & Bain Limited, Glasgow, Scotland.

For Sarah

ACKNOWLEDGEMENTS

Some of these poems first appeared in *Poetry London*, *Magma*, *Nth Position* and *The Shuffle Anthology* (2008). 'Downsizer' won the Essex Poetry Competition in 2005. 'Night Signals' was commended in the Wigtown Poetry Competition 2005. 'Flat Dad' was commended in the National Poetry Competition 2007.

I would like to acknowledge New Writing Ventures for their support in 2006/2007. I thank Esther Morgan for her advice on many of these poems, and I also thank A.B. Jackson and Ahren Warner for their help with the manuscript. Special appreciation goes to Roddy Lumsden for his invaluable insight and generosity.

Above all I give my love and gratitude to Sarah Harrison, Asher and Suki.

CONTENTS

Mountain Man

Hot-wired bears have foregone the berry,
ripping car doors off at night, prankster jocks
crashing through the brake on a candy high.

They pace their dens to a tight sugar clock,
and lie all day in the tall grass,
scratching at their dusty coats, idly tracking

long threads of milkweed butterflies.
Here and there he points out evidence
of ursine peaks and troughs.

He sets to showing me how to coax
a rag of flame from a nest
of shredded juniper bark... *Pay attention!*

But the forest scent, its list of bitters,
recalls me to the seam of moss pinched tight
between the paving slabs back home:

the velvet folds where Little-Boy-Green
has caught his princely britches,
fleeing to the underworld.

Grand Union

After a night of lasers, and one
outsized glitterball
scattering its hoard of coins,
what else to expect
but this muffled aftershock
and the canal lying like a pulled ribbon
beside the industrial park.
A questionable gift.
We jockey its leaden pulse
at a moonish pace,
the ground upholstered beneath
our exhausted legs.
The morning sets out its collection
of long, withdrawing shadows.
The xylophonic echo
of bicycle wheels over loose flags
plays somewhere ahead.
It's when we hit the backs of houses
that we find our first angler,
hooked up to his silent telegraph,
dreaming of lips rising to light.

Red on Maroon

It was to the frisky comb and Rizla buzz
of 'Cross Town Traffic' (in a town
with a five minute rush hour)
that you tried, beneath Rothko's
'Red On Maroon' (1959), to turn
a hobbyhorse into a thoroughbred.
All that effort to see your half-
formed work race off towards
the first available gap in the fence,
the report of confluent hooves
flicking their diminishing *da-da-dumb*
staccato over the hedge line,
taking their frolicsome horse-play
decidedly elsewhere.

Dolphin

Alone with the secret stuff in the parts store, I heard a noise
like the grub of a bullet being dropped into a kidney bowl.

I held my eye to a cold strip of air, watched as you slid in
like a credit card through a lock, the bone glow

of your lab coat moving past the tables, swelling behind
the bell jars and demijohns. Any second the dozing lab might

come to with a flutter of strip lights. A room dreaming of itself.
A mix of cutting-edge and Victoriana: oak panel and tiled ceramic,

centrifuge and waxy parquet, fume cupboards and terminals,
the glass faced cabinets full of specimens whitening in liquor.

You made for the slab where the dolphin lay, black rubber
in the bad light, its smile reminiscent of... is it Gary Sinise?

Someone who is, perhaps, not taking you seriously?
I've seen that smile on so many faces. A wry line scored

with a thumbnail. You stood in front of it for a long time,
arms folded, considering the signature wave of the dorsal fin,

the body fat as a radio valve. Then five rapid punches,
the breaths between each hit tight as a prizefighter's.

My eye was weeping from the draught, my nose tightening
around the stink of formalin. I couldn't make you out.

In the morning they will find the five indents still there,
clustered to the side of the babyish forehead, the necrotised

skin and blubber holding the shape of your knuckles
like a mould; the smile evolved into that of a martyr.

Higgs Bison

Most of what has been attached to my name should not have been
JAMES HIGGS

It treks the stilled pulse of sap,
the tangled cabling under a lawn
where the root has outstayed the tree.

It sneaks across the faded denim of a lung,
picks apart the marrow, is couriered
by kidney and liver from bar to bar.

I've caught scent of it in the alkaline bite
of circuitry that hangs in the air
long after the blown moment has passed,

felt its shape within the heart's baste of threads
that tightens with each beat,
its longing in my hands, jaywalking

from collarbone to breast, the tripped-
over morse of boundaries long gone.

The Night Studio

There's no such thing as an unintelligent painter. It's an anomaly
PHILIP GUSTON

On a night like this,
when the lobby porters are dozing
before walls of pigeonholes

and dangling keys,
and herds of late traffic still bleat
along 5th Avenue,

I imagine him suspended in the darkness
above the garment district,
the only clue to his industry

the glowing slab of a skylight.
Strip lights on chains,
the rattle of a turpsy brush against tin.

There's always the urge
to throw in the towel, to slip out
and join Franz, Bill or Mark

at the Cedar Tavern
and trash another night.
If the studio were to tighten

around one event it would be this:
chasing an image as it shrinks back apace
into the dark from where it came.

And always the hand,
the soft commutator of the brush,
threatening to push it further away.

Telescope

Nautical, for catching sails on the horizon,
or Fab Four semaphores,
or ensigns strung like natty smalls.
Nothing that comes within its range
benefits from its supposed X10.
The moon shakes unchanged in its lens.
I lift it in hope of opportunity
the advent calendar opposite might offer up:
a curtain teased open with a thumbnail,
spilling a tungsten-lit scenario –
gaudy deliverance from the cold blue
seance light pulsating tirelessly
Friday–Saturday night.

Flat Dad

I'd taken out the bones so that he
might settle into a lazy S
that would flatten over time. Unless
draped, as now, across a bench,
or hung, yesterday, from a tree.

Wherever I choose to rest and release
the weight of him, I am careful
to keep intact the parted tuft
of soft white hair.

I pitch camp and taste
the lichen edge of billy water,
bite into a stale crust,
the sound internal of the jaw
working loud as feet through snow.

In the fly-cast drift, the hour-line
played out between my fingertips,
I wait for the river to tighten.
In the silence between each breath,
birdsong – hesitant; lacking a confidence
that will return, perhaps when I am gone.

I collect myself and shake him out
in a slow wave, watch the crumbs scatter
and the dust rise, and, shouldering him,
move on to the next town.

Writing from the Imperial Three Star

My image archived face to face and back to back
in curved, green tinted lines as far
as these mirrors can conspire
to power themselves,
I ride the elevator with its three mirrored walls –
a walk-in voicebox calling out the floors,
a bowl of light above me
with its shadow-load of dead flies,
the trim seam of buttons
beside the brushed steel door,
floor numbers set out in no nonsense numerals,
each embossed with a pucker of braille.
That voice back home would be RP.
Imagine the client going through the specs,
choosing the exact tone to extract that mix
of deference and desire
from each susceptible employee.

In my room, two cast-iron radiators,
byred to the wall like drowsy techno cattle
and starved to the bone,
are drying out my travel suit
and patient brogues.
Hospitality stamped on pillowcase, towel and soap –
the hotel's outrageous crest.
A font some big-sleeved lover might strike
for breathless technicolour love.
It's been so long since I demanded
elegance from an actual pen,
a bright sheet of paper, my tangled script:
People just don't bother anymore – writing, like this.

Bikini

It's hard to believe that Fleming
had Cary Grant in mind,
saw him, not Sean, part foliage,
eyebrow banking over a wry smirk
as Ursula examined her latest conch.
It's strange that when I think of bikini
– try as I might to think of somebody else –
it's my mother who always comes to mind:
a mint-green swimming cap
blistered with tiny roses;
a yellow two-piece with ersatz skirt
sewn tight around her soft paunch;
the weak swell of water ahead
of her patient stroke.

The All Night Service Station within the Heart

Sometimes the furred tongue fails the work,
just lies there, underwalked and overfed,
barely raising its wet tip
as the simple words flicker over
and fly out into the world.
Their outsize Letraset sticks messily
to both referred and unreferred.

And deeper in, a tetchy heart
tut-tuts through uneventful hours, cousined
more to the stapler than the cricket,
more to the metronomic tap dancer
who slowly drips his regular step
across an unfurnished stage.

But now we've moved from sound to spotlight
or rather the skirt of light
beneath the bathysphere
which is, in fact, the all night service station
within the heart,
sleeping with its bright eye open
and its jaw relaxed, waiting for the soft roll
of rubber on forecourt.

Blinkers

After rain: the dull romance of waiting.
With luck the sun breaks through,
a city of glass slides free of stone
and the road itself becomes a mirror –

each walker a miracle of foot
upon counterfeit river.
So many faces are made young
in this uplight, made beautiful.

I shade my eyes from below,
and, as if gesture is recondite cue,
my bus rounds the corner.
Time enough to pat my pockets

for an unleavened wallet.
The doors part, the driver regards me
as a squire would from his horse –
raises his beanie, invites me to board.

The Rolodex

I knew things had changed
when he shushed me to take the call.
I stared at my hands, the soft box joint
of interlocked fingers, thinking how
once we had been close, in that
wounded fashion like skinny dancers
huddled over cigarettes.

The retro-gift I'd given him years ago
still sat on the table, smoked plastic
flip-lid, semi-opaque, the blades
of the index cards clearly visible.
I watched his fingertips,
their little bitten-down hooves,
moiling through his contacts, fetlocks
stained with tobacco –
back and forth, back and forth.

Bush Craft

My father rolls a worry stone
within the blackout of his trouser pocket.
He brings it out into the light, its toffee hip
worn to a waxy slide by his iguana thumb.
He lets me handle it, its shape
proof of each rubbed thought.

Our picnic blanket is half his jacket
and half *News of the World*,
the crackled fossils of two boiled eggs
and a Rizla twisted around a pinch of salt.
Have you heard of origami?

He turns his scarf through bewildering folds
and pulls it taught to form two breasts.
He lies back, one arm folded behind his head,
and lowers a roll-up to his smirking lips,
the cotton paps still draped across his chest.

22

Sade

The car rocked as you twisted and reached
into the back to get your rucksack,
the stiff leather of your Zegna jacket
creaking with each movement. We were

close enough to see the polished brass number,
the frost sugaring the steps, the dags of hardened
mud and leaf hanging from the boot scraper.
You were fiddling with the lens cap,

your cigarette flicking up and down as you spoke,
flakes of soft ash falling into your lap.
I was admiring the shaky dexterity, how
your hands knew their way around every

facet and tweak of your sacred Leica –
that lucrative third eye – when I noticed
a sheet of light racing across the opening door.
There she was, standing on the icy threshold,

as if summoned, rubbing both arms against
the cold and looking up and down the street.
What did she make of us, not waving
but wiping our breath from the windscreen

in a muffled panic, the flash going off
inside the cab? We missed her retreat,
so smooth and quick; just the click
of the door jamb swallowing the lock.

Leading Man

So small he sits on the edge of my palm
with his back against my brandy glass,
legs crossed, relaxed,
diminutive glass in *his* hand.
But this is just the play of parallax,
sitting, as he is, on a bolster
on the other side of the room.

He's had enough banter
with his band of admirers.
Now they've drifted off to examine
the party's exposed machinery.
He saunters over with a Fosse skip,
sprung thighs, caffeine pulleys
working away from shoulder to hip.
Twenty clap press-ups just for me.

He dabs the back of his reddened neck
with a neatly folded serviette,
says he wants to prove how a look
touches as much as the hand.
In the garden, I squint one-eyed
at my fingertips as we run them over
the gelateria of evening cloud.
The pinks, he says, *the plum and ash.*

He steers me across the fescue lawn,
toward the drive where he's parked up tight
between two smoked-glass limousines.
He points the fob and the stalled notes
chirrup like pebbles over a frozen lake.
I'd like to tell you what Stanley thought,
I mean really thought, about that scene.

A Star Is Born

To observe your diktat
would have been a courtesy.
Yet still I turned up, half-sunk
beneath the Plimsoll line
of canapé and free champagne,
to disrupt the ceremony.

Local Sauce

An octopus can stream itself
through a ragged peephole
punched through metal or glass
and emerge unscathed the other side;
can use a screwdriver,
or bottle opener – if it so chooses –
adopt the colour of any flag,
enormous forehead
like a blow-up academic's,
furrowed by deep philosophy.
And though I have bitten
into the tough frill
of a juvenile tentacle
and tasted nothing apart
from the local sauce,
I have witnessed a dogged
tenderness that taste alone
could not impart, how,
in Kardamili, I saw one spire
itself around a fisherman's arm
as he unloaded the jumbled trove
of fish and crustacean from a boat
hung with drying sponges.
When he prised it free,
and dangled it like a piece of lingerie,
I could see the black beak
snapping in muted song,
a deflated ink sac somewhere inside,
its contents emptied and eased out
to transparency by the tide.

Geneva

When this tram-viola has passed on its stubby wheels –
wing bone sprung against the elevated wires –
I'll call back across the zones.

You'll ask,
Have you been thinking about me at all?
I'll reply, *Of course.*

Right now I'm watching the cup I've set down
aquaplane across the wet table top,
an inch or so before it comes to rest.

I goad it with my spoon.
But it's found its rationale,
suckered, limpet-tight, to formica.

Part of a worldwide second wave,
I've spent the morning sat on the terrace
with nothing else to do but watch the crowds

spider like marginalia along the Rue de Rive.
I want to lower my lips to the table
where I've drawn the line

of your shoulder from the pooled rain.
But the waiter's eye is on me,
slick as a peeled lychee.

Lichen

Scarfskin on corrugated asbestos –
if ever you've climbed up there
as I have, keeping to the roof-spine,
careful of the brittle sheets,
the wired glass skylights.

A doily graft of antique guano
mapped over brick and doorstep.
It scratches at the palate, brings
summer's hebetude to mind,
the days fragrant with worked sisal.

Diamonds

You find them roadside –
drifts of shattered safety glass –
where staved-in windows
spill frosty constellations.
I remember how you tried to trade
for a lucky bag, presented a palmful
of ragged hail to an amused shopkeeper.

Such plans we made, foundered
on the hard edge of wakefulness.
It was in poor light I left you,
still sobbing beneath your parka hood,
the rabbit trim I coveted.

Stuff

It's with the ornamental bridge –
the cutest of handles – I lift this pond,
its lily-choked brilliance,
putative carp caught somewhere
between glimpse and absence.
Now I'm left with no means to cross
to what remains of the long evenings
we'd lie together in murmur and shade

But there's other, house-bound stuff
to kick-start memory:
your things gone, or rather,
mine thinned by the absence of yours.
I flick through the wardrobe.
Its soft zoetrope replay the years.
There's the jacket to ward off bores;
the ruffed shirt that made me invisible;
the row of shoes, your chorus of lovers.

Family Tree

Not the regular advance of thinning tributaries
bearing an impossible weight of names,

the graft-work of tidy marriages.
Mine would be fat at the waist,

wayward and heavy with leaf and shy fruit;
two magpies careful not to split

their luck and tangle with my comely locks
as I reach for the golden goose.

The Full Kit

Even before his brother had counted a hundred,
he'd taken himself up to the flat roof
and laid his duffel coat over the frosted lumps
and pleats of tar and settled himself
beside the black plastic attaché case.
The gutter at his elbow sagged
with gutter moss, dense and quaggy,
the nose drawing out its supra-bitterness.
He caught sight of a napless tennis ball
being suckled by the downpipe that had choked
on the peaty slick of its own blockage.
He fingernailed the moulded clasp,
fingertips as alive to the cold as exposed bone.
All that broken down glory –
the chamber, the barrel, the telescopic sight:
all laid out in faux red velvet.
He could feel the slight camber of the roof
against his flattened body, the slope
that would shrug off the rain, or have
a ball roll down into the moss-lined guttering.
He snapped and screwed it all together –
a beautiful logic outside instruction –
thumbed twelve grey bullets into the magazine,
heeled it home, then turned the silencer
until it tightened on the snout.
He settled down to wait, only the tip
of the silencer and the cloud of his breath
betraying his position.

A Sloping Pitch

Was it butane or propane, Gaz
or Triangia? I can never remember
that kind of detail. I do recall
the air heat-wavering like water
above the stove, the ring
of neat blue petals splaying so
compliantly beneath the kettle
and how it had been an uphill struggle
to sleep: someone tearing long strips
from the dark with their snoring,
cars returning late, and the sloping pitch,
the yaw of the ground rolling us together
as if all night rounding a corner at speed.

Retro Ascent

Bar the flight and the hotel bus,
this time he's gone for old-school,

roped monkishly to his guide,
a slow climb through thinning air.

Each time they stop for breath, his eye
sips at the silverplate of altitude.

By Mallory's standards they travel light,
for the body should consume

something of itself in the journey.
Tonight's repast: mint cake, oatmeal, cocoa.

Then the careful stowing of breeches,
woollen socks, waxed cotton;

the creak coaxed out of leather
with finger-dabs of foggy dubbin.

Their clattering tent – a sky lantern –
glows as the mountain darkens.

A dip nib, worming for script,
pecks at ink frozen in its bottle.

He'll ease it loose with the warmth of his hands,
imagining her under an age of lace,

not the quick jeans and halter top
that carry her through summer back home.

Attic

Morning dabs its bread at the window,
trying for the rough-cut meat
of faux Tudor beams.

This room rises from its own mist,
we the draped monument, each detail
tweaked under a directing lens,

our clothing dropped
into sniggering piles of import,
the things that hold us up and in.

My tongue's spittle glaze has flexed
and cracked under word and flesh.
I rise from our republic of linen

to press my face to the glacial pane
and check my thin-boned bicycle's still chained,
shivering, to the railings below.

Mr D.

Some fall mid-stride, the sprung chord
that runs through the bone snipped in two.
Others find themselves alone beside
the unattended console of night,
where here and there a few lights
burn on into the early hours, waiting
for the morning to rise like floodwater.
Some are excellent, vanish
inside the mouth like candyfloss.
Some leave an aftertaste:
esters of ambition and decline.
But you are different, tough
as a bolt against my teeth;
a dying battery on the tongue.

From the far-off vantage point of adoration,
to the tight maze of your fingerprint,
I have picked my way through
macrobiotic barricades
of alfalfa and buckwheat,
forded the lazy swell of blueberry smoothies,
lost clear form beneath the dodge
of coffee and calisthenics.
But over-tightened surety
merely buckles the seam, tempts the finger
to worry and pick.
This is close work now.

Night Signals

Just as Jodrell Bank intercepts the discreet sobs
of pulsars from the padlocked
basement of the stars,

spectacles and fillings in remote arctic towns
pick up the curtain flutter
of the Northern Lights as dirty sound.

And while the grass blade, tweaked
in innocence, is the hair spring that trips
the owl down to the kill, this twitch

tugging the corner of my eye is not
the self betrayal of a frayed nerve,
but a suture being tightened by a nurse

in A&E, the pinstriped consultant at her elbow
the on-call specialist from thaumatology
who full-moons a stream of pebbles

under his skin, to reshape into this waiter
who palms the shift of dust
from a plum black bottle of wine,

inclines and rotates it for our approval.
You taste, give a purse-lipped nod
to his withdrawing, double bow,

and lean back in your chair
as I dip forward to speak,
the movement a signal for the bartender

who's calmly ramming the throat of a glass
with a towel, giving me the eye,
to turn the music up again.

Downsizer

Your breath, its bitter tone of stale tobacco,
comes back to me again this morning
as I rake up the selfsame tang of wet leaves,

dry-smiling through lips thinned
into a mere suggestion of contentment.
You would always be the first to drape your coat

over the broken glass of a perimeter wall,
pulling me up, as if my smaller hand
had emerged, gloved and shy, from a carriage.

Squeezing onto another dark site,
you had a fox's eye for loose corrugation,
a nose for never-seen security guards.

Then the celebratory cigarette – bent
and damp, hard to light – before raiding
the builders' hut for eggs, for the egg fight.

With your hairless chest and catgut laugh,
the charcoal smudge of your first soft moustache,
what would you have made of the lime glare

of the local tennis courts, floodlit tonight
beyond this wall of black cypresses,
the steady chock-chock of the big hitters?

Wildflowers

Either I'm losing sight of you,
or there is something wrong with my eyes.
The eyes we developed to

such a fine pitch I could pick out
yarrow and knapweed
in a teeming meadow.

The Tea Chest

Simple, unadorned orthodoxy of the practical –
where craft outwits money
by a generous stretch –
he'd brought it home
to house the growing overspill,
its plywood panels smooth
and droughty to the touch,
the battered metal edging
punctuated with rivet dimples
like excavated pelf, tarnished
and earth-flattened.

Mornings you'd get the pungency,
bled all night into sleep-moistened air,
the grey-scale of dawn giving accent.
Gritty filings of tea got everywhere,
left flea-like smuts on the skin.
We'd feel it in our mouths,
between our teeth, the tongue
chasing tough grains across the palate.

Once he turned up half-cut, flushed
as a glassblower from the steep climb,
coat pockets stuffed with balls of newsprint
where he'd slipped away
with a few ceramic figurines.
He teased them open on the kitchen table
as we gathered round,
tea leaves falling from the creases
as he worked through the crumpled layers
to get to the cold slip of light
on milk tooth porcelain.

New World Guest House

Bangkok, beyond the triple glazing, is mute.
The air-con would keep an hour fresh for days.
With mineral water I wash the fruit:
the plums, the grapes imported from The Cape.
I rub my thumb into the soft lanugo
of two fat peaches. *It's tap water*, you say,
stepping from the power shower,
hair stacked inside a beach towel,
its fuzzy map of the world twisted
and tucked beyond recognition.
I examine the label: *Mont Fleur*.
Snow-capped mountains, foothills in flower,
the plastic shot with an alpine tint.
I raise to my eye the frosted transparency of a grape,
roll between my fingertips its propagated jade.
A flash of towel and you are frisking tresses
between India and Canada.

8 - 0

Red turtleneck, flesh-toned tights.
Her white skirt ripples like a cuttlefish.
He comes alongside, keeping pace,
takes her hand, holds it high as if she alights.
They brace one arm each behind the other's back
and take off between the tenderfoots.
He wears black, sports a devil's goatee.
Outside the rink the earth tugs against their fluency.
You strike out alone, leave me clinging to the side,
score a perfect figure-of-eight across the soapy ice,
then slip into a big fat zero. I'm thinking ahead
to the flimsy cup and the ribbon of coffee
that drop from the vending machine.

Clean

A crowd of young men and women has gathered
in the field across from the Baptist Church.
Vows of chastity are being exchanged.
You establish this with a slow-tracking dolly shot
as you cycle past: the *woo-hoos* and *yeahs*
of witnesses in their casual wear; the couples
kneeling face to face, sparkly and clean as
licked pebbles, mouthing inaudible words.
The season underscores all of this: daffodils
drying out into chewy strips of flex,
the grass excited into thickness by the Local
Authority mower. Then it comes back to you,
her father's disapproving face, rising up through
the *ohs* and *ahs* – the soft vowels.

Provenance

This girl, applied thick as whipped cream
to a square foot of buckled canvas.
An artist's hand has reached the limit of its range –
a confluence of vapid eye and synaptic dithering.
I'm turning it over and over,
searching for a date or signature.
The work of an amateur. Or perhaps
something more accomplished – an advance
through the stages of a great unlearning.
She brings in two cups of sweet tea,
a dial of oatmeal biscuits on a willow-pattern plate.
There is no provenance as far as I can see.
Then the silent stir and slow dunk.
My uncle had brought it back, *Along with those*,
she says, nodding to the mantelpiece,
the huge mirror faltering through damaged tain.
I finger the jumble of medals and curios.
A pair of wire spectacles with the glass gone.
A sheathed dagger, rusted now, refusing to pull free.

Y

Your fruit-stall colours snag the eye
of the bored receptionist as we hurry out,
the locator signal of your sandals
clacking off through the darkening lanes.
I take it easy, lag behind and watch
your tanned calves shake with each step
as we climb the Moorish ramparts to look
out over the half empty star-field below.
We detect the odd spark of a farmhouse,
the clusters of deep sea light
where other villages happen,
the distant flow of headlights and tail lights
on the highway that led us here.
In the morning I'll be stretched out
on the bed, staring at the Y
where ceiling and corner meet.
You'll be sat up, stroking the guide book,
lips following the text,
searching for *the stunning ravine*,
which we will find after *el desayuno*,
full of abandoned white goods and furniture.

Pro Rata

A burst of light like a slap in the face –
as if a gavel has woken me, or a wheel-
barrow's tipped its sluggish load
with one testy jerk and is suddenly light
and wayward in my hands.
This same low sun that strobes through the carriage
is searching your desk right now,
igniting whatever it finds.
That's where I place you, your body grown dark
against the luminous gas of twilight.
I chart your lost features automatically,
make leaps of rendition where knuckle
and elbow are stepping stones.

The scrunch of my feet on the path.
Your pet name for me across my shoulders.
It drags a hackling tail, takes playful bites
at the flinching skin of my neck.
The intruder light sets off its sodium flare.
Your weekend squeeze is here again
with his month-old key that still feels
as if it could shatter like glass in the lock.

The Lawn

It really is his half-acre; the sharp borders,
the sprinkler swinging its beaded lariat.
He keeps to himself, wishing me gone.

Sometimes I catch sight of him behind glass,
slotted between a reflected garden
and a muted house, one hand sunk

into the soft depths of a cardigan pocket,
the other holding a pipe on which he huffs,
and puffs – gilled – unreadable.

The Bite

Little mammal, you burn with the cold,
breath as grey as leaf pyre smoke.
Gladly I sit at the end of the quay

and watch you whiten the black water
with fitful strokes, coax you
from struggle to something surer.

Where so much care resides in the mouth,
I bite down lightly, lift you out
into a towel embrace.

If

And then she half-turns
at the school gates,
regards you off-the-cuff,
her body suddenly still
against the home-time rush.
It makes you giddy
as a first-time steeplejack.
But it's more than enough for
another term, another year even,
in which to rehearse your opening
gambit, to close your hand
over your skittering heart.

Boy with Cat in Harness

The light is not the only thing rifling through
the communal gardens.
The boy walks over fallen leaves

as if over glass or some other giveaway debris
whose noise has drawn me to the window.
He has a cat in harness,

the sketchy black leather almost wanton
against marmalade fur.
I can picture his mother helping him

pick it out from where it hangs
with the other mini dom-wear
above the chewy sticks and retractable leads.

The garden has risen up through waves
of leaf and rain, and I can look straight down
between the skinny shanks of trees

at the rose bushes with their tight buds
and the rope swing next door's children
helped their drunken father toss

and tighten over a branch that seems too thin.
Each time I watch them swing I hold my throat
and wait for the branch to give.

It never does, nor will.
Such strain and elastic purpose.
As with this boy, overseeing the tugs and pounces

with immoderate jerks of the lead
and what must be a wicked tightening at the neck,
the nose and paws jabbing and searching

through wet grass and copper foil leaves.
That such anxiety and constraint
should put love away from harm.

Sunday

Flicking through the choppy wake
and counter-wake
of the clockwise-only slow lanes,
past faces puckered
above the froth of meagre strokes,
I am at one with my dolphin brothers
and sisters, their fish-for-tricks
melancholia.

And afterwards, the showers.
Straight in, straight out,
while others soap
their naked selves like cars.

Triumph Dolomite

After the cattle grid, the cream of macadam
gives way to pot-holed gravel.
The ground has re-tightened

over what the rain had loosened;
tyres grumble over tailings
and cat o' nine ruts.

We're looking for the *old places*,
unchanged skerries floating among the swatches
of ploughed and unploughed land.

Fat stitchwork primps his driving gloves,
leather supple against his skin,
his hands held at ten to two as we slow,

clocking me in the rear-view through a cloud of panatella.
She dials a stuttering fix on pat-a-cake Jagger,
demanding *Satis faction*.

When the rain comes the wipers flail
like something stamped on, and the windscreen
is as lost to sight as a droppered eye.

Circus

Life's slow abduction leads to here:
a room, a desk, a counter.

We will free you all from your strip-lit cages.

The words that will march, trunk to tail,
down the street one day.

Single Lens Reflex

Back then I'd spend an age setting up the shot,
an old school Pentax SLR,
dense and lustrous as a chunk of coal,
the weight of it in my hand
something I might casually throw.

I'd wedge it with a few twigs and stones,
nudge its heavy jaw until I'd got everything in,
set the timer and make my way over.
But it's a blur now: the poses you threw,
the faces I made; the light squeezed
through a tightened aperture.

Oh Yes, Yes... I Think I Can See it Now

You pull Love's *Forever Changes*
from a battered sleeve
that tightens with each re-sheathing.
You can never get enough of that
West Coast fusion of sociodelic
and mariachi fanfare, where street corner
meets Tijuana brass.

Lowered into the microgroove, the stylus
orbits in towards the same end-surf
as that picked up by the VLA, New Mexico,
where laid-back plotters and archivists of stars,
of the abraded silences around each star,
look up and out each night,
making their fine adjustments.

En Plein Air

I showed my son a small painting I'd made
when I was sixteen years old. My first attempt
at oil on canvas, the canvas glued to cheap board
rather than pulled across a stretcher. He went
up to his room, bearing the ten inch
by eight landscape with exaggerated care,
the woods that inspired it long since
altered by the sequenced grip and flare
of seasons. Our plan is to find
the spot where I'd set up the mayfly-legged
easel twenty-odd years ago. I've got the date
written on the back in my awkward hand,
a location fixed loosely in my head;
a recollection that it was cold and getting late.